WELCOME TO

YOSEMITE

NATIONAL PARK

BY PAMELA DELL

Many thanks to the staff at Yosemite National Park for their assistance with this book.

MAP KEY

The maps throughout this
book use the following icons:

🚗 Driving Excursion

🥾 Hiking Trail

⛺ Campground

🏠 Lodging

🔭 Overlook

✴ Point of Interest

🧑 Ranger Station

❓ Visitor Center

🌲 Wooded Area

About National Parks

A national park is an area of land that has been set aside by Congress. National parks protect nature and history. In most cases, no hunting, grazing, or farming is allowed. The first national park in the United States—and in the world—was Yellowstone National Park. It is located in parts of Wyoming, Idaho, and Montana. It was founded in 1872. In 1916, the U.S. National Park Service began.

Today, the National Park Service manages more than 380 sites. Some of these sites are historic, such as the Statue of Liberty or Martin Luther King, Jr. National Historic Site. Other park areas preserve wild land. The National Park Service manages 40% of the nation's wilderness areas, including national parks. Each year, millions of people from around the world visit these national parks. Visitors may camp, go canoeing, or go for a hike. Or, they may simply sit and enjoy the scenery, wildlife, and the quiet of the land.

TABLE OF

The Child's World®

**Published in the
United States of America
by The Child's World®**

PO Box 326
Chanhassen, MN 55317-0326
800-599-READ
www.childsworld.com

Acknowledgements
The Child's World®: Mary Berendes, Publishing
Director

The Design Lab: Kathleen Petelinsek,
Design and Page Production

Map Hero, Inc.: Matt Kania, Cartographer

Red Line Editorial: Bob Temple, Editorial Direction

Photo Credits
Cover and this page: Darrell Gulin/Corbis

Interior: Corbis: 6–7; Bill Ross/Corbis: 14;
Darrell Gulin/Corbis: 13; David Keaton/Corbis:
10; Don Mason/Corbis: 17; Galen Rowell/
Corbis: 1, 9, 22 (top), 22–23; Geoff Renner/
Getty: 18; Marc Moritsch/Getty: 26–27; Phil
Schermeister/Corbis: 2–3; Phototake Inc./
Alamy: 25

**Library of Congress
Cataloging-in-Publication Data**
Dell, Pamela.
  Welcome to Yosemite National Park /
by Pamela Dell.
    p. cm. — (Visitor guides)
  Includes index.
  ISBN 1-59296-704-3 (library bound : alk.
paper)
  1. Yosemite National Park (Calif.)–Juvenile
literature. I. Title. II. Series.
  F868.Y6D435 2006
  917.94'470454–dc22   2005030069

On the cover and this page
El Capitan (at far left) towers above
Yosemite Valley. At 3,593 feet
(1,095 m) high, El Capitan is a
favorite with rock climbers.

On page 1
As the late afternoon sun hits
Yosemite Valley's peaks, the beautiful
colors are reflected in Mirror Lake.

On pages 2–3
The mist from Yosemite Falls helps
wildflowers of all kinds grow
and thrive.

WELCOME TO YOSEMITE NATIONAL PARK

∧

🚶🚶

A Man Called Muir

Yosemite National Park

CALIFORNIA

Welcome to Yosemite National Park! You won't be disappointed by your visit here. The spectacular views are never-ending. The climate is mostly mellow and mild. The park is home to hundreds of different kinds of plants and animals. Few other places on Earth include so many different kinds of **habitats** in one location.

Through the efforts of people like John Muir, Yosemite became America's third national park. In 1868, Muir left San Francisco and journeyed southeast, mostly on foot. He walked through wildflower fields that grew waist-high. He crossed streams and rivers. He kept going until he reached the foothills of the Sierra Nevada mountain range.

There, nestled on the California side of the Sierra, Muir found Yosemite. Native Americans had already been living here for years. Muir's lifelong love of Yosemite would later benefit millions of others, too. Yosemite became a national park in 1890. Today, Yosemite's many wonders are protected for all to enjoy.

The Greatest Californian

In 1976, the California Historical Society named John Muir the Greatest Californian. His work and his writings still inspire nature lovers everywhere. Muir founded the Sierra Club in 1892. Today, that organization has more than 750,000 members. The club helps people understand the importance of respecting and protecting our beautiful wilderness areas.

John Muir (MYUR) was born in Dunbar, Scotland in 1838. When he was 11, his family came to the United States and settled near Portage, Wisconsin. Muir traveled to California in 1868, and eventually married and settled down there in 1880. Muir died in 1914 at the age of 76.

Yosemite Rocks

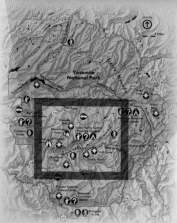

Do you like big rocks? Yosemite is the place to see them. Yosemite Valley is a good place to start. Yosemite's granite is made of five different minerals. This gives it a salt-and-pepper variation in color. Hike across the granite to see this effect up close. The minerals include quartz, hornblende, biotite, and two kinds of feldspar.

These silent rock giants form part of the western face of the Sierra. They give Yosemite its very special place among national parks. Together, they tell an ancient story. The granite first formed deep within the earth, millions of years ago. Over time it was uncovered. Forces inside the earth pushed the land upward, creating the Sierra Nevada range. **Glaciers** formed. As the glaciers moved, they scraped against the mountain surfaces. Slowly they carved into the granite. What remained were these cliffs and many unique rock formations.

These rocks now form the amazing backdrop of Yosemite Valley. Some of their names are well known, like Glacier Point, El Capitan, and Half Dome. This huge, world-famous granite dome sits at the east end of Yosemite Valley.

Nature's Mild Side

Long, sunny summers are Yosemite's specialty. However, nature shows many moods here. Thunderstorms, forest fires, and floods sometimes occur. Snow flies every winter. The climate changes from the lowest elevation to the highest. The Sierra forms a barrier that keeps out harsh weather from the Pacific Northwest. Rain clouds passing over the peaks get caught. They pour their water on the plants and animals. The west side of the Sierra stays cool and moist.

If you come to Yosemite from the west, you will pass through woodlands. Summer is hotter and drier in these low foothills than anywhere else in Yosemite. Winter snows are rare. Mice and other rodents are common, as are skinks and other lizards. Bobcats and bats can be found in these foothills, too.

As you wander under oaks and pines, listen closely. You might hear the tapping of an acorn woodpecker. Look for the manzanita, with its reddish limbs and red berries. These shrubs were important to the region's Native Americans. They used its berries for food and dye.

As you climb higher into the foothills, you reach Yosemite Valley. Here, winter sometimes brings a great deal of snow. The higher you go into the mountains, the longer and fiercer the winter. In the spring, the melting snow swells the region's rivers. Plants and trees start to grow. The climate is one reason that Yosemite is home to such a **diverse** range of living things.

Scenic Yosemite Valley

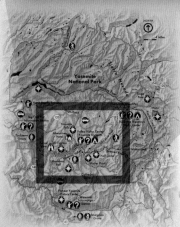

Yosemite Valley is the place where most park visitors begin their adventures. A wild world stretches out around you. The Merced River winds lazily through the meadows and fragrant forests. The fresh scent of evergreens you smell comes from the sugar pines, incense cedars, and Douglas firs that grow here. You will probably see plenty of gray squirrels in their boughs. These squirrels live in most parts of the park. It will be hard to miss the mule deer, too. They **forage** throughout Yosemite. Other animals are harder to find.

The Lost Grizzlies

One animal you will never see in Yosemite is the grizzly bear. Grizzlies once roamed this wilderness. Then people hunted them until there were no more. Mostly, this hunting was for sport, and because the grizzlies were dangerous. California's last grizzly bear was shot in the 1920s.

👣 Yosemite Falls is made up of three parts: Upper Yosemite Fall, the Middle Cascades, and Lower Yosemite Fall. Altogether, Yosemite Falls is 2,425 feet (739 m) high. The best time to see the falls is in May or June, when melting snows bring greater amounts of water. By August, the falls are often dried up.

High above you, the white ribbon of Yosemite Falls tumbles down the granite cliff. In the spring, even from afar, you can hear it thundering. Sometimes it is so powerful that you can feel its mist from a distance. Yosemite Falls drops in three separate sections. Measured all together, they make the longest waterfall in North America.

From the green valley floor, you will also see a huge, lone-standing slab of granite. This awesome formation is El Capitan. It is the world's largest granite **monolith**. It challenges the most experienced rock climbers. Get close enough, use binoculars, and you may see some of those experienced climbers trying to reach its peak.

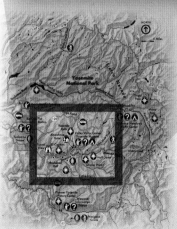

Sky-High Cliffs and Conifers

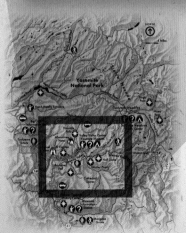

Yosemite Valley covers only a small area of this vast park. Surprisingly, 95% of Yosemite's visitors never venture farther.

Did you notice the giant overhanging rock on the valley's south side? This is Glacier Point. If you think you can stand its dizzying heights, a trip here is essential. Once you are there, you may think you can see forever. Far below, Yosemite Valley now appears to be a miniature world. The vistas stretch out all around you, and many different waterfalls can be seen. Glacier Point is one of the most breathtaking spots in the world. It is fairly easy to reach, too! Red fir, western white pine, and Jeffrey pine grow in the Glacier Point area. Put your nose close to the bark of a Jeffrey pine. You will probably smell vanilla or butterscotch!

A mountain climber descends from Glacier Point. The point is a favorite viewing area for visitors, as spectacular views of Yosemite Falls, Vernal Falls,

Mariposa Grove contains about 500 giant sequoia trees. One tree, called "Grizzly Giant," is believed to be almost 2,000 years old. It is thought to be Yosemite's oldest living sequoia.

Near the park's southern border is another amazing world. Here, you enter a dense forest. The smell of pine tells you that you are in the midst of conifer trees. Conifers are evergreen trees. They stay green all year and have needles and cones. White fir, sugar pine, and ponderosa pine stand all around you.

These pines are tall. They will seem like dwarf trees once you reach the Mariposa Grove of Giant Sequoias. This is the biggest and most impressive of Yosemite's three sequoia groves. The sequoias here have been standing for more than a thousand years. They are some of the tallest living things in the world. Most of them are almost as tall as a 30-story building.

These forest giants are protected now. In the past, many others were cut down. This left only huge, flat tree stumps.

High Country Meadows

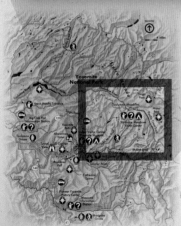

Tuolumne (TWALL-uh-may) Meadows, on the park's east side, is your next stop. The most scenic way to get there is by taking the famous John Muir Trail. Along the trail, which begins in Yosemite Valley, you won't cross a single road. But you will walk through deep forests, down into valleys, and up again. You will pass crystal clear mountain lakes and more granite cliffs. On your way, look for wildlife of all kinds. One to watch for is Yosemite's rarest and most **endangered** bird, the great gray owl. Everyone wants to spot this hard-to-find **predator**. Few ever do. Black bears may be easier to find. Don't expect them to always be black, however. They are actually often brown, blonde, or even reddish in color.

Rare Alpine Wildlife

You will have to climb above the tree line if you hope to see Yosemite's one endangered mammal species, the Sierra Nevada bighorn sheep. The sheep roam in the highest mountain peaks. There are only about 30 of them in the herd, and the best place to look for them is around Mono Pass.

Underwater Valley

A scenic wilderness area called Hetch Hetchy sits on Yosemite's western border. It was once a beautiful valley. Today, the valley is entirely underwater. In the early 1900s, San Francisco's government wanted to dam the Tuolumne River to create a **reservoir**. Such a reservoir would provide the city of San Francisco with water and electrical power. But it would also put everything that lived in Hetch Hetchy Valley underwater.

John Muir fought a long battle to save this beautiful region. In the end, he lost. Today, the San Francisco

Tuolumne Meadows sits high in the sub-alpine region of the Sierra. Because of the wet climate, fewer trees grow here. If you come at the right time of year, however, the wildflowers will reward you. They blossom in brilliant colors during this area's short summer. One look and you will understand why these meadows were one of John Muir's favorite places in the world. Stop at the Tuolumne Meadows Visitor Center for clues for telling the plants apart. These meadows are important for the survival of Yosemite's mountain beavers, willow flycatchers, and other animals, too.

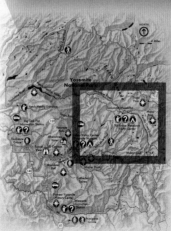

Moon Magic

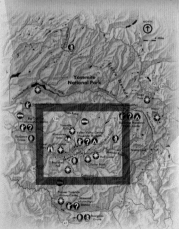

Night has fallen in Yosemite. Sitting near Yosemite Falls, you are ready to rest in nature's arms. The sky above you is splashed with a million stars. A pine-scented breeze tickles your face. The hoot of a great horned owl carries eerily through the trees. A howl comes from somewhere in the distance. It is a sound that makes you shiver. But stay put! You are about to witness an awesome sight.

As the full moon rises over the roaring thunder of Yosemite Falls, magic seems to occur. Do you see it, arching across the frothing waters? Look for a band of rainbow colors. These colors glow against the night's gloomy shadows. You are seeing something few people ever do—a mysterious **lunar** rainbow. Sometimes, if the moonlight is especially bright, you might see a second rainbow, too. The moon's light sparkling on the foaming, crashing waters can bring these rainbows to life.

Lunar rainbows are sometimes called "moonbows." Just as sunlight passing through raindrops or mist causes rainbows, moonlight can have the same effect. But the moonlight must be very bright to make moonbows—they only occur when the moon is full or nearly full.

Finally, you return to your campground and settle into your sleeping bag and say goodnight. Nearby, the lunar rainbows create a soft nightlight, watching over you as you sleep. When you dream, you will probably dream of this wonderland called Yosemite.

Camping in the park is certainly the best way to see its nighttime beauty—but be sure to make plans ahead of time! Camping is a very popular park activity during the summer months, and you'll need to plan ahead in order to save your camping spot.

VISITOR G

27

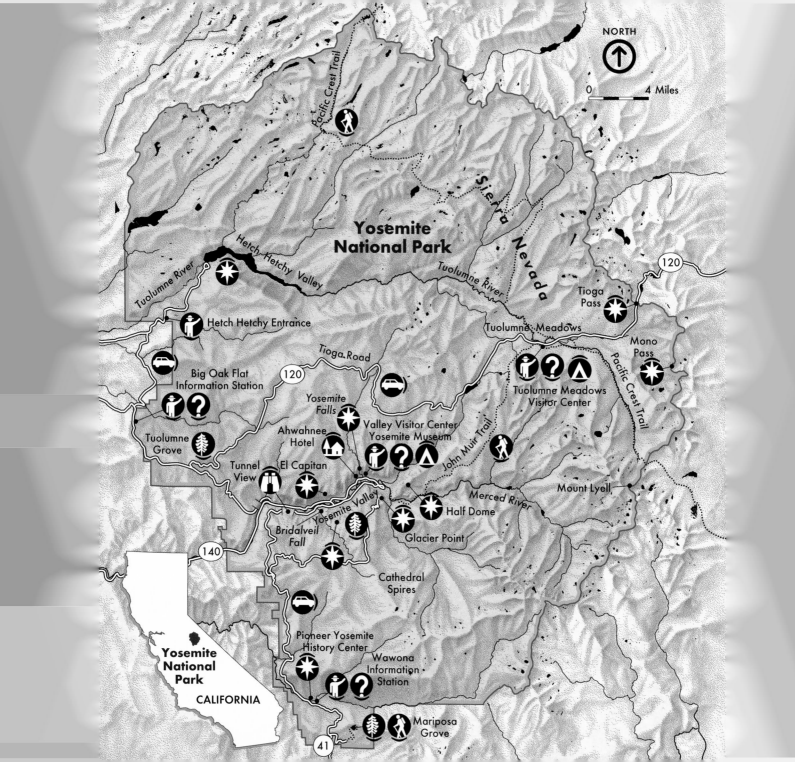

NORTH

0   4 Miles

Pacific Crest Trail

Yosemite National Park

Sierra Nevada

Hetch Hetchy Valley

Tuolumne River

Tuolumne River

120

Tioga Pass

Tuolumne Meadows

Mono Pass

Hetch Hetchy Entrance

Tioga Road

Big Oak Flat Information Station

120

Tuolumne Meadows Visitor Center

Pacific Crest Trail

Tuolumne Grove

Yosemite Falls

Ahwahnee Hotel

Valley Visitor Center
Yosemite Museum

John Muir Trail

Tunnel View

El Capitan

Mount Lyell

Merced River

Yosemite Valley

Bridalveil Fall

Half Dome

Glacier Point

140

Cathedral Spires

Yosemite National Park

CALIFORNIA

Pioneer Yosemite History Center

Wawona Information Station

Mariposa Grove

41

YOSEMITE NATIONAL PARK FAST FACTS

Date founded: October 1, 1890

Location: Central California

Size: 1,169 square miles/3,028 sq. km; 748,160 acres/ 302,770 hectares

Major habitats: Forest, sub-alpine meadowlands, rocky slopes, low-lying marshes

Important landforms: El Capitan, North Dome, Cloud's Rest, Half Dome, Cathedral Spires, Glacier Point, and Sentinel Dome

Elevation:
   Highest: 13,114 feet/3,997 m (Mount Lyell)
   Lowest: 1,800 feet/549 m

Weather:
   Average yearly rainfall: 35–40 inches/89–102 cm
   Average yearly snowfall: 62 inches/157 cm
   Average temperatures: 89 F/32 C to 25 F/–4 C
   Hottest: 98 F/37 C
   Coolest: 26 degrees F/-3 C

Number of animal species: 77 kinds of mammals, 242 species of birds, 40 kinds of amphibians and reptiles, and 11 species of fish

Main animal species: Mule deer, California ground squirrel, gray squirrel, golden-mantled ground squirrel, coyote, black bear, Steller's jay, blackbirds, raven, a variety of woodpeckers, and red-tailed hawks

Number of flowering plant species: 1,400

Number of tree species: 37

Most abundant plant species: Pacific dogwood, ponderosa pine, California black oak, black cottonwood, lodgepole pine, ceanothus, manzanita, California lilac, bluegrass, needlegrass, and hairgrass

Number of endangered animal species: 11—including Sierra Nevada bighorn sheep, mountain yellow-legged frog, Yosemite toad, great gray owl, willow flycatcher, peregrine falcon, and southern bald eagle

Number of endangered plant species: 5—Congdon's woolly sunflower, Yosemite woolly sunflower, Congdon's Lewisia, Yosemite onion, and Thompson's sedge

Native people: Miwok and Paiute

Number of visitors each year: About 4 million

Important sites and landmarks: Ahwahnee Hotel, Tuolumne Meadows, Yosemite Falls, Bridalveil Fall, Nevada Fall, Vernal Fall, Ribbon Fall, Horsetail Fall, Tunnel View, O'Shaughnessy Dam (at Hetch Hetchy), Sentinel Bridge, Yosemite Museum, Yosemite Cemetery, and Miwok Indian Village

Tourist activities: Hiking, boating, canoeing, water rafting, fishing, horseback riding, mountain climbing, wildlife viewing, snowshoeing, cross-country skiing, and downhill skiing

GLOSSARY

diverse (dy-VURSS): Things that are distinctly different from one another are said to be diverse. Yosemite's alpine meadows contain an extremely diverse number of wildflowers.

endangered (en-DAYN-jurd) When a type of plant or animal is endangered, it is in danger of dying out. Yosemite's bighorn sheep are an endangered species.

forage (FOR-uj): To forage is to wander in search of food. Many animals travel to different regions of the park as they forage for food.

glaciers (GLAY-shurz): Glaciers are huge slabs of ice that move, and are created when many layers of snow get packed together into ice. Millions of years ago, glaciers carved out Yosemite's rock formations.

habitats (HAB-uh-tats): The places where animals and plants are normally found living and growing are known as their habitats. Great gray owls and bighorn sheep live in two very different habitats in Yosemite.

lunar (LOO-nur) Lunar refers to things that have to do with the moon. In Yosemite, you can sometimes see a lunar rainbow—a rainbow that occurs in the moonlight.

monolith (MON-uh-lith): A monolith is a large rock formation that stands by itself. A monolith like El Capitan is easy to see because it stands alone against the skyline.

predator (PRED-uh-tur): A predator is an animal that stalks other animals to kill and eat them. The mountain lion is a fierce and effective predator.

reservoir (REZ-eh-vwahr): A reservoir is a manmade lake created to store water for any of several different uses. When the Tuolumne River was dammed, it created a reservoir that wiped out many plants and animals.

TO FIND OUT MORE

FURTHER READING

Halvorsen, Lisa.
Yosemite.
Woodbridge, CT: Blackbirch Press, 2000.

Lasky, Kathryn and Stan Fellows (illustrator).
John Muir: America's First Environmentalist.
Cambridge, MA: Candlewick Press, 2006.

Muir, John, and Joseph Cornell (compiler).
John Muir: My Life with Nature.
Nevada City, CA: Dawn Publications, 2000.

Petersen, David.
Yosemite National Park.
New York: Children's Press, 1993.

ON THE WEB

Visit our home page for lots of links about
Yosemite National Park:

http://www.childsworld.com/links

NOTE TO PARENTS, TEACHERS, AND LIBRARIANS:
We routinely check our Web links to make sure
they're safe, active sites—so encourage your
readers to check them out!

INDEX

🚶🚶 ABOUT THE AUTHOR

Pamela Dell's writing career began in fifth grade, when she wrote and published her own monthly magazine. She then graduated to short stories, usually featuring various classmates as characters. As an adult, her first paid writing jobs included advertising copywriter, technical writer, and entertainment journalist. In 1990, Pamela began writing for children, and since then has published over 40 children's books (both fiction and nonfiction). She has also created award-winning children's interactive multimedia. These days, Pamela hangs out mostly in Chicago, Los Angeles, and San Francisco.